Cassells, Cyrus.
More than peace
and cypresses

MORE THAN PEACE
AND CYPRESSES

Cyrus Cassells

COPPER CANYON PRESS

ACKNOWLEDGMENTS

Kudos to Sol Waters for his assistance, and to Greg Blaine,
Mike Wiegers, and Ken and Peggy McIntosh for their support.
Greg Bailey welcomed me home to Rome after half a decade, initiat-
ing the swift, surprising current that formed this "book of heroes."

Some of the swatches of gypsy lyrics in "Black Sounds, Black Sounds
(The Possessed)," and "Little Ballad of the Moorish White Town"
are from Tony Gatlif's beautiful film *Vengo*.

My gratitude to the editors of the journals in which these poems
first appeared: *Borderlands*, *Gulf Coast*, *The Indiana Review*, *James*,
Ploughshares, *Provincetown Arts*, *Salmagundi*, *Tex!*, and *Wild Plum*.

Printed in the United States of America.

Cover art: Giorgio Morandi, *Landscape*, 1913. Oil on cardboard,
41 × 55 cm. Courtesy Museo Morandi, Bologna, Italy.
Photo: Luciano Calzolari, Crevalcore, Bologna.

Copper Canyon Press is in residence under the auspices of the
Centrum Foundation at Fort Worden State Park in Port Townsend,
Washington. Centrum sponsors artist residencies, education
workshops for Washington State students and teachers, Blues,
Jazz, and Fiddle Tunes festivals, classical music performances,
and the Port Townsend Writers' Conference.

LIBRARY OF CONGRESS CATALOGING-IN-PUBLICATION DATA

Cassells, Cyrus.
More than peace and cypresses / Cyrus Cassells.
p. cm.
ISBN 1-55659-214-0 (pbk.: alk. paper)
1. Americans — Europe — Poetry. 2. Fathers — Death — Poetry.
3. France — Poetry. 4. Italy — Poetry. 5. Spain — Poetry. I. Title.
PS3553.A7955M67 2004
811'.54 — DC22
2004007133

2 4 6 8 9 7 5 3
FIRST PRINTING

COPPER CANYON PRESS
Post Office Box 271
Port Townsend, Washington 98368
www.coppercanyonpress.org

IN MEMORY OF MY FATHER, CYRUS
1933–1999

AND HIS BROTHER, NORMAN
1943–2004

᠄

In the roiling world,
the elms of all you were
anchor me.

Contents

PART I

Handlebar, Night Face, Moon,
Summer Dress

PART II

ﾆ

A Blue I've Found
Only in Andalusia

PART III

༄

More Than Peace
and Cypresses

I knew a man who'd sweep the roof and clean the skylights and railings only out of gallantry towards the sky.

LORCA
The Public

PART I

⌁

Handlebar, Night Face, Moon, Summer Dress

Wind of the Appian Way

More than peace and cypresses, emboldened
larks in the olives, I love
the jetsam beneath the upswept pines, the brokenness
along the ancient Appian Way.
As I amble, toppled pillars,
timeworn pedestals, the scattered
jigsaw of no longer
champion Latin,
a row of stone patricians fingering
their immobile togas,
heyday gone, faces,
greed-swayed plot and denouement —
enough to glean
the god of this once reigning
queen of Roman roads
is a disheveling tempest, an Ares
of smithereens —

Now a lark-sudden cusp
of sunflowers, whip-smart senators,
a yellow quorum —

Now a bas-relief
broken off at the arms,
the throat:
the upright tribune's
lantern jaw and harnessed eloquence
deleted, deleted —

Here comes the x in extinction;
the wind, not Caesar, decides
what's supernumerary:

all that seemed central
confiscated, winnowed, dropped —
like coins or orphaned
feathers in a well.

Local Train

after Montale

It was like this, like the gusty
shudder that ruffles
the too-staid suburbs
and hurls the day's ash
up to the treetops,
like the roughhouse wind
bending, assailing the willows,
spinning the clueless weather vanes —
it was this way, a blitzkrieg
of rain ambushing
the poppy fields, the fluttering
wash on the lines,
bursting pell-mell through
the unshuttable window,
and the triggered stranger,
the other passenger and I
letting it happen, loving
the downpour: the fat, mirthful
drops spattering our sleeves
(bedlam!),
and, just as quick,
inescapable,
at my neck, the shock
of his slick-combed,
coruscating hair (Caio,
his name was Caio),
his rain-flecked lips;
in his stevedore's terse, swiftworking fingers,

the first unruly blue button,
then the rest —
till, in time, a supplanting,
an invigorating wind, redolent
of salt and blossoms,
rose through the jammed window,
teasing my drenched
nipple, my nape, the revealed
caduceus tattoo along his torso,
fanning the seat with its alloy
of rain and semen.

Like a match-flare,
you whisper, *like a shudder* —
pressing the cool stem of a venetian
glass to my nape —
like this?

Ferragosto

Umber and baled wheat:
from memory,
I have Massimo's blondness
(hay-stack messy in the morning),
Almir's "gi-raffish" grace;
from memory, the moon-filled bed
(Did we snore?
Did we sleep at all?),
the laze-awhile bed we shared,
first as chatterhappy,
steadfast friends —
hours of wine and gossip
and Massimo's ubiquitous guitar —
and then as *più che amici*
(more than friends),
gleefully named
after a novelty act:
I *Gatti Acrobatti.*

Dear Mystery, once I spotted
my straightaway kin
in the obstinate heat
of emptied Rome,
my wayfaring men,
near the water clock
in the leafy Pincio,
tell me why
I never left their sides,
their summer-borrowed rooms, save

to fetch clean clothes;
why, for an addled week
and more (the vacation week
named Ferragosto),
my Neapolitan doors,
my revered windowsill that faced
the ancient wall of Rome —
bonanza of stone and light —
became nothing to me.

Ferragosto:
the dog days shimmered,
and the clattering traffic thinned,
letting us rovers reclaim
the sound of broom straws,
the ocher of buildings,
the salmon of the venerated city again:
that pink.

I remember the Roman holiday
turned our arms and legs
to a forest honey,
and once, while combing
the stock-still streets,
sunstruck, inseparable,
we discovered, near the Spanish Steps,
a troupe of mesmerizing
acrobatic cats:
I Gatti Acrobatti —
There was a miniature
leaning Tower of Pisa
metamorphosed into a cat's perch;
costumed cats crossing

an arresting tightrope,
and for the finale, the blustery,
scarfaced impresario
chose Almir and me
from the dazzled crowd
to hoist two glittering gold-leafed poles
as Alissa, the fleet
show-stopping cat,
leaped back and forth,
blithe as a triplet.

Later, after countless wolf's-hour toasts
to a host of things, including
the agile, mercurial cats,
there was Almir,
more than a little soused
and hot to know —
You're gay, aren't you?
Guess you figured Mass and I
were a couple —
what it felt like with a man,
and Massimo confessing
how he and another swimmer once…

Did it really happen?
Their novices' kisses
and uproarious horseplay:
Just which pole, they teased,
like the cat Alissa,
are you planning to leap onto? —

Did it really happen?
Almir on the phone from Rome

this crisp morning—
Almir who's become
the spruce father of three
rambunctious girls, the friend
who still calls me *Gatto*—
weeping, telling me
Massimo's body was found:

Massimo, caught in an undertow—

I close my eyes,
dear Mystery,
and there he is,
with a careworn, slightly
nicked guitar,
a clove cigarette:
umber and baled wheat
the Roman summer turned to butter...

I Dream the Death of Cesare Pavese

Frost, then mausoleums of wheat,
coal-dark and stillborn grapes —
Anti-mandarin, avid
for revelation, he dares
to write of the lurid,
the harsh and fallow life:
lowborn whores,
blighted peasants,
stark threshing-yards and bereft
yellow sheaves,
women in inert black unlatching
dilapidated shutters.

Questing, fugitive, the poet moves
through the piedmont's
sinuous and sprawling kingdom,
worrying a single line:
The midwives come running, fast.
But whose birth is this?
Whose death?
For him, the cobalt of the mobile
watercourse below,
the earth seen from the belvedere,
the slope,
is a seizure;
human pain robs
the riveting vineyards, the Langhe hills
(the sun-enhanced hills which are
the hermit's pride)

of their clarity:
No words. An act.
I won't write anymore.

This is subtraction: delectable figs
pilfered, effaced,
unsparing scythes obscured
first by phantom summer
then autumn fog.
Suddenly, the land is sheeted:
now his palm is white
with pills —

Yes, the poet and the land are sheeted...

The Death of Vincent van Gogh

I. THE MAELSTROM

The martial yellow of the field,
the sullying, ambushing wind and wheat:
foundered priest, indefensible apostle,
he knows each thing he sees
will become a heresy:
crows like brigands, brusque
Saracens on the canvas,
a green and russet road
through the vehement wheat.

In Auvers-sur-Oise, July's
belligerence, merciless July's
muzzling heat:
above the wheat rows, the open country,
the lantern-stern sun,
menacing, unjust, and God's
all-suffusing elegance,
the valley of Adam
not findable,
the shrewish pistol shrieks,
not here, not here:

one shot for the washaway scarecrow,
carrot-maned, ugly, impolite, sick —

Red boot prints,
ceaseless, arduous —

The brigand crows take wing, take wing;
the mountebank crows take —

Coal-hot and auburn pauper,
he lumbers back to the village,
ransacked, unraveling:
red palms, red pittance —
the land, the downfall yellow, and the day
his maelstrom.

The room at the *auberge*, imagine,
where he dragged
his unmistakable wound,
his unlodgeable bullet —
oh, to have botched
even that, even the pistol that seemed
deadsure —
too stifling —
the olive cupboard in the corner,
rock-silent, and the meager skylight
with the iron latch —
too abject to contain
this sonata of unremitting
love and failure,
this utter hammerfall —

And to Theo, deftly, devoutly
lifting the untameable painter's
ever-present pipe,
bless him,
the now discarded life
of his horizonless brother
is like Troy glimpsed
through suddenly abating smoke —
now carnage,
now beauty,
now carnage —
toppled, eviscerated Troy...

Someone has placed clementines
on Vincent's grave —
in winter, delicate and reverent.
A little January sun,
gold reveille, illuminates
the stones of the incautious,
fiercely devoted brothers,
buried a mere six months apart.
A bed of ingratiating ivy
is eager to engulf
the slightly lichened markers;
a busybody, almost unbridled green
seems intent on devouring
Theo's dates, their double Calvary.

Through the plow-lined,
frost-ribbed winter field,
returning from the cemetery,
for the poet, there is the slap-
obvious, required
crow in the road — the Dracula sheen
goes through me like a shot —
and time to imagine the field
in coercive summer,
the reddened hand, the roiling,
premonitory wheat.

Years ago I knew a painter,
wrenching, doleful —
I don't know what became of him —

a young beast, perennially
spattered with paint from his upstart,
sin-eating palette,
and everywhere he left
small tsunamis of pain,
so that my soul would wince
on seeing him,
his shadowing,
milquetoast whippet, Charlie,
an emblem of his skinlessness and terror.

Always, always I feared for his life,
and what I felt, I imagine,
was a little like what Theo endured
with his whirlwind brother.
Can you understand?
Can you remember the alarmed and alarming
friend, the blighted,
uncontrollable rebel who confirmed
the fragility of the universe,
the maverick whose insurgence
was a page of fire
from the book of heroes,
the pariah,
whose coffin is carried past you now
through the village of Auvers,
as if by crows,
ring-leading crows! —
something deafening, unregenerate in the air —
and you in your black hat, black,
cumbersome jacket,
just beginning to discern
the true, indispensable allies,

the faithful —
Lord of Vincent,
what's the apt blessing, the least
harrowing farewell? —
from the mountebanks,
the fatuous collector, the impervious
charlatans in mourning guise:

Mother, life was such a burden to him
but now, as often happens,
everyone's full of praise
for his talents.

Revelatory, stricken, unsaveable yet saved
by scrupulous sight:
He was so much
my own, own brother.

The Shepherd of the Villa Caffarella

adjusts his earphones,
as the sheep range around him
in the Roman sun.
I am an apprentice of umber
light and shadow in the villa,
and I know him a little
from my walks.
Usually we talk of the quotidian,
soccer or weather,
amid brambles and voluble belled goats,
constellations of Queen Anne's lace.

On villa land, he has shown me
a ruined columbarium
from the days of Constantine,
and a sacred grove,
inundated with daisies.

Once he led me — the villa
emerald again after winter —
to a grotto adorned
with a nymph's statue,
headless, voluptuous, agile.
The water in the ornamental pool
shimmered. The dusk was freaked
with the little upended
exclamation points of poppies,
and there was a pulse,
a thread between us,

rife with waiting.
But we grew fainthearted,
afraid to touch,
as if some shared holiness
might be defiled.

Still, our soft-natured, sustaining
friendliness prevails,
undeterred.
And like any beautiful and commanding thing,
the shepherd of the Villa Caffarella
is uncapturable,
transfixing as the infant
Moses drifting among
the astonished reeds —
or a red flash:
a pheasant in the grass
near the grotto.

Au Revoir (The River Again and Again)

And the Paris of my childhood hopes
became the real Paris,
the navigable Seine — a swift
litany of sculpted bridges,
a wintry odyssey of bridges;
glimpsed garrets blued with screenlight;

and, come inspiriting spring,
greengrocers, voluble cafés, the wild-hearted
traces of mooncalf kisses
all over the tomb of Oscar Wilde
(whose exquisite handiwork?).

Before you, unbeknownst to you, always
cached in my breast pocket,
the canny Magician from the tarot,
as if I had summoned
the silver dollars from your sleeves
at Yann's soirée, summoned

your wonderland atelier
with its brash, alluring woodcuts
that brought to mind
Rilke's lauded Orpheus:
All becomes vineyard, all becomes grape,
ripened on the hills of his sensuous South.

On the steps of Sacré-Coeur,
over my uncapped head,
you christened me with a madcap

ribbon of champagne,
as the hoped-for and dreaded
millennium blossomed,
and the colossal crowd became
a galaxy of chanticleers.

I want to say: with you,
I was immeasurably alive,
regal magician,

that once I woke and spied
two Adams in the mirror,
windowlit, entwined:
myself surprised by myself,
but with a guideboat
clarity and calm.

Yet all these glints, these minutes,
are the Paris of the past,

as now, by the moon-flecked river, I unwrap
the painting you left me —
you who were upright
then gallant in your wheelchair —
like an *au revoir* in oils, a hallowing
last letter:

And in helmeting moonlight, Cyrus,
there by the blue and pewter
body of the Seine —
river that embellished our coupling,
moon that clothed us in pearl —

did you read it?

24

What Is This Life an Eel or a Poet Has?

for Eugenio Montale

All the way from Vernazza to Monterosso,
past unforgiving shoals,
sea-flash and sun-pinked flesh,
past a choir of cliffs, a hurrah
of wheeling blackbirds,
the wind's inanities, the wind's disfavor,
the initiating eel rested,
languid in my hand,
burnt match still murmuring
its misspent, its implied crimson —
and the eel was you, Eugenio,
black, tractable necklace,
elfin shadow,
and the lemons,
and the locomotive sea,
all you —

Sundown:
from the palisades, the crucible
headlands of Cinque Terre,
in human form once more,
you culled at last
the plummeting sun's ray,
bolstering, elusive, countinghouse green —
in my boundless dream,
your keen soul, your iris cradling,
for an unstoppable instant,
the swift supernal.

Exile, guardian of limits,
poet in your skullcap
of crushing memory,

I have prayed for this for you.

Atavism

after Pavese

To feel the sultry ghosts
of the ancient city —
Rome, avuncular Rome —
on his skin,
like pine silt,
to let his eyes snare
the illustrious owl,
the nighthawk's plunge,
the barely checked boy
beneath my lids,
the moping boy striped
by stifling shutters,
the unstill dauphin,
the unbarred dreamer,
would step out under the night-cloaked
porticoes, the upraised pines,
without cargo or decorum,
without hampering clothes —
who owns the street? —
unfettered as a brindled cat.

Moon, rallying moon,
tell him I understand
his barbarous urge
to soak up the indolent
night's cool.
Masterless sea,
tell him I understand.

Once, from a lumbering streetcar,
I saw at dawn —
as the rails curved
away from the Colosseum —
for one onerous moment,
a naked woman,
gimcrack and pitiful,
near the track —
No, not like hers,
not shamefaced:
so help me,
the boy's nakedness would be
almost prayerful —

Easy-footed, unkenneled,
the boy beneath my lids would collapse
the purblind barriers between
night and flesh,
eye and shooting star,
to know again
the power of his birth hour —

In the villa of his pipe dreaming,
where the midsummer air weaves
a make-do toga,
Chiron, the rugged tutor, the muscular
stone centaur, wakens
and walks
with no misgivings,
and now, animate, with open relish,
the stone bull,
who is unbridled Jupiter,
begins to low...

The White Road *of Giorgio Morandi* (1941)

Pale as Sicilian almond milk
in summer,
and as soothing —
I have only
this underprized path,
an antidote
to puffery or dismay,
an antidote to Black Shirts,
wolves, and the brazen
machinery of war.
Road of the dove's breast,
the hoisted truce-banner,
road of the craving for peace,
mother-of-pearl path,
usher me again
past the three sun-loved,
ambitionless houses
whose walls hold
the greenish, the inferred
gold of olive oil, the jailed gold —
past silvery junipers,
witnessing foliage,
lush bystanders who seem to laud
the blessings of austerity,
the trio of poplars,
the fostering cypress:
Lord, I know them as I know
my own hand,
my smeared, quixotic palette.

Today my tall-masted, wayfaring anima
requires only
these small, ancillary steps,
anchoring left then right —
Who am I?
Who am I now? —
the mind bleached a little
of invasive terror, of capsizing
diffidence and regret,
the mind, so often
regimented, machine-rigid
as *Il Duce*'s Rome.

Look, the sky is a milky
and amassing blue —
Beside the path, pale as sugar,
the familiar cypress will turn
dark as cassis.
The first headlong stars
will be Virgils.
The world will howl,
bullying, pugnacious —
lust and marksmanship,
lust and carnage —
but the dusk will be kind,
fleshy and cool as peonies,
thick with the monastic whispers
of telltale leaves,
ministering branches,
and I'll get where I'm going;
I'll find the peace,
the holiday-making white roses
you mentioned long ago,

dear brother,
dearest sisters,
the inviting jasmine —
even as the rapacious night,
with its hunter's beard,
its black and blush-red gloves, grips
the earth outside Grizzana,
falling as slack-jawed
poverty falls on the world,
I'll be found at last,
deep in a boa of fragrance.

The Courtyard at Via Fondazza

for Giorgio Morandi

Not enough — one palette,
one praise-song
to convey the contours, the syntax,
the super-subtlety of the courtyard.
What do the roofs say?
What do the roofs reveal
of this day, this dream-bitten
human epoch?
Not enough, not enough,
one canvas for the dogged
or besotted eye,
so that you have to capture it,
Morandi, in every season:
in vigorous spring, the allotted branches
khaki-colored,
then prehensile, bare at Epiphany;
in a serene, sedulous
series of oils,
a lover's unrelenting gaze
to insinuate an illusory
kingdom of glimpses;
how little we can cull
of our neighbors,
the wind-stirred whites and fidgety blues
of the fluttering laundry on the line,
maybe the only clues
to the courtyard's intermittent actors,
the seldom seen:

a precipitous flash of nakedness,
or a supper-smeared apron...

If you stare at the memorized walls long enough —
the regal, tantalizing crack in one
like a handle —
they may confess to you
whether they're consoling
or imprisoning —
or just part of the proscenium,
soulless as porridge,
the rudiments of some everyday opera;
they may confess
dismay or indifference.

Morandi, I remember
my own courtyard,
with its un-ignorable March and April gifts
of wisteria and swallows,
how the intricate chess of light
and shadow on the ocher walls
somehow soothed and obsessed me —

And my neighbors?
Almost all of them remained
a mystery.

In those years, the eye-catching apricot
in the courtyard
became my cicerone,
my steadying, venerable companion,
and in voluble spring,
I waited avidly

for its white utterance:
in Roman sun,
the glory of the loved and the received,
and then, as always,
the deft, ensuing
pull of the unknowable.

I was a clue-loving,
flaw-loving detective, Morandi,
on to the hint of the universal
in the succulent terrace aloe,
the swatches of other lives,
the just-born blossoms.

Wild to Be Seen Again

for Philip and for Jean Follain

They come back — out of what blue? —
the little clay-bottomed jugs
we were given in Céret, suffused
with a local lavender;
the serene medieval statue's face
that surfaced — *make room! make room!* —
as we helped Michel
dismantle his kitchen wall,
all of us dumbfounded —

The demure souvenirs (emblem
of our forays in the Pyrenees, our first
escapades in Europe),
where are they now, Philip?
On the bureau, their fragrance endured
even beyond our holiday.

I hear our beach-hound suitors
imploring, calling after us
(in Perpignan, in the languid, prodigal
summer of 1983),
and my teasing reply:
"Even *gens de couleur* get sunburned!" —
And there it is, the old
mordant question of God:
Lord, just what did you intend,
letting our youngblood lust
and laughter burgeon
in the thick of a plague?

I have only hearsay,
Philip, that you may have died
in a Hawaiian hospice.
They come back — out of what blue? —
your crash-into-me eyes
(the copper of a pocketed
lucky penny),
your dancer's verve and heroism,
so that now, after so many
immuring years,
mourning's cascade can begin
in earnest — *make room! make room!* —
the contours of your face
like the kitchen statue:
trenchant, resurrected, wild
to be seen again.

Elegy for Giorgio Bassani

What I recall is a shoring, replenishing
Roman meal:
river-cool wine and fine
olive oil and cutlery, and you
casually remarking
that you first came to Luigi's rousing tables
in 1944,
jolting me with the razory
hem of the words
when I was in hiding —
the cat's cradle
of what it meant to be
not the brute
but the yellow-starred, the cornered —
so at the news of your death,
dapper creator,
master builder,
I'm flooded with
how fully we are all kin to
the fragile and myopic
Finzi-Continis, your fictional
Ferrara Jews.

Giorgio, when the predatory, the remorseless
comes for us
(yes, beneath green friars,
confessor olives,
in the garden we have

an appointment with Judas),
how unprepared we are,
how unprepared.

The Two Deaths of Pier Paolo Pasolini

I found an early poem in your dialect
that brought back
a trip through Friuli,
the vermilion and derelict peach
of the burgeoning morning
as my train neared
Slovenia and Croatia,
and the ache from the poem
(like the memory of the morning land
and the later-cauterized Croatia)
was the distance between
the hushed, inconspicuous end
you envisioned as a young man,
and your Kabuki-wild, inelegant death —
you, with your encyclopedic sense
of transgressive paths,
fathomless desire, and poverty;
you, the uncensored night's and the slums' advocate.

Poet-hunter, the rumor is
you cruised every sundown of your life:
the last, the very last time,
on the seashore drive,
the "trick" was alluring
but barbarous —
And you, famished boy,
are you a lover
or just one of the shelterless
werewolves of Rome? —

a formidable foe:
a butcher's son wielding
a bone-smashing board.

Then the Judas kiss of the tires' concussive
back-and-forth over your body,
the *ragazzo di vita* in the transiting
silver sports car,
your blood lamp-black beside
the sea's unchecked gallop.

In your young poet's dream of death,
choirlike, the crowns of the lindens
grow cryptic.
Under a boulevard's April branches,
in the ardent yellow you've just left,
intent on home, a boy
is a guileless comet's tail
as he darts from school in his gregarious
helmet of curls.

Sun-shaft or moon's arrow, the light
and the hurrying boy
go on without you,
Pier Paolo…

August and Everything After

after Pavese

October:
gravity and annulling wind pinioning
the limbs of the fruit trees,
the glinty olives;
the cannon-gray dawn auguring
a long, lax day of rain —

Where once a young god breathed,
whose footsteps astonished the earth,
whom Viking sadness touched
hardly at all,
like a cloud's frail shadow,
now, at the windowsill,
a man with his scepter
of anxious thought,
hair and once-supple arms silvered —

In August, he thinks,
the beach-browned idlers, the reveling passersby
had a meaning;
in surefire summer,
nobody died.
Maybe someone faltered
and was nursed —
in the plague time? —
but there was always the young god,
glamorous, affable, immured

from death,
who lived for everyone,
and was anodyne:

the air no longer
quickens at his breathing —

As if dust-whitened, deconsecrated,
you wake one morning,
and the summer's dead,
but your eyes are still threaded
with the sea, the immense, truculent
light of August,
and in your ears,
dear God,
the roar of the sun
changed to blood —

Handlebar, Night Face, Moon, Summer Dress

for Bernardo Bertolucci, after a viewing of *Luna*

He mistakes the moon's curve
for his mother's cheek —
handlebar, night face, moon, summer dress —
as she ferries him
(in his Book of Genesis, the earliest
of all his memories)
on her elating bicycle
in the voluminous dark
beside the shore.
And the elements of that mesmerizing night
become the whole scheme, almost
the whole story —
and the impact
of a sun-swabbed morning among the mute
toy trumpet, the pert beach ball, the stock-still
glass of milk,
when he dribbled a thin beam of honey —
marionette string —
and his hovering mother
licked the sweet mistake
from his leg,
while the agile shadow of his shoeless father
subsumed the tiles,
carrying a piquant crate
of fresh-caught fish
to be slit, to be gutted —
Then chaos:
his mother and father dancing a twist

in the flooding light
that looked bellicose
(the father frisking, teasing the mother
with the knife and a glittering fish),
and the bedeviled cub he once was,
wailing, lips mussed with milk, snared
in his winsome grandmother's
intricate yarn,
trailing a long, pallid kite-string of it
across the terrace.

And I have a stake
in this stark vocabulary —
honey, mother, fish knife, tangled yarn —
like an inadvertent Sherlock
stumbling onto secrets,
for I first saw the boy
with his genial skateboard,
loving, savoring the Janiculum Hill,
then later, aghast, I found him,
at wolf's hour,
near the turtle fountain
in the Old Ghetto,
eyes fluttering, a strident
needle in his arm.
Who is this galling, handleless boy
who speaks of himself
in the third person:
At thirteen, he started using
H, the hard stuff —
How did the honey become
the ogre of heroin,
the complicated yarn become

an anaconda, a chalk line
on a crumbling, piebald wall
that leads me, like a curious,
whistling urchin,
to the strung-out junkie boy's lair?

When did the fish knife become
the cutlery — *this can't go on* —
the deracinated boy
uses on his arm,
insane, insane,
when he's orphaned
of his transporting needle,
so that his mother has only,
at a tumbledown hour,
the moon's curve of her breast,
her hand on his sex —
what would you undertake
to keep your son alive? —
to lessen his ungovernable withdrawal.
This can't go on:
so, as he sleeps off his shuddering,
she puts on his clothes —
they fit — a boy's
sea-colored shirt and jeans,
and enters his surreptitious world,
a discerning spy,
to secure his fix, to bribe
his young, flower-faced
Moroccan friend and dealer
to keep away.
And she has a weapon in this war:
the slatternly, the medusa yarn

45

of the long-cached fact
of who his father really is;
so they set out,
mother and son,
on the old roads
of her put-aside past:
she drives the snared boy
to his birth father's door:
it is an odyssey
as bracing, as tantalizing
as their first bike ride together
under the moon.

Tell him he needs his father,
who is barely legible
in his memory,
a shadow on the tiles.
Tell him he needs
Giuseppe's acumen, his fish knife
to help sever the yarn, the hunger
that could leave the boy
key-cold as a gutted,
gleaming fish,
in some pigeon-gray Roman alley.

Let the moon become at last
her opera veil
that she covers him with
while they weep
at the father's revealed
identity and return,
so the annealed boy becomes
like a ray himself;

the veil he filches from her
as horseplay, the white
of her billowing dress
long ago —
handlebar, night face, sea sound,
summer journey —
becomes more of the gibbous moon
above him,
or the magnum beam
from her bike,
adept, assiduous,
that pierces the voluminous
night of his first memory.

Vesuvius as Sleeping Beauty

We had stopped to collect
windfall figs, a few
truant or crimp-backed flowers;
at the placid edge
of Signora Aponte's venerable
garden on Capri,
Vesuvius as Sleeping Beauty,
boatlights like glittering foil
employed in nubile vineyards
to deceive the starlings —

You held the wild, surviving
lily to my face.
Suddenly we were more than
distinct, adjacent solitudes.

Suddenly I was filled with the dark
amber of the island's singing.

PART II

A Blue I've Found
Only in Andalusia

The Soul before the Great Mosque of Cordoba

al-Andalus —
you had only to utter
the open-sesame of its name
to deftly conjure
heart-fortifying tiles,
bewitching fountains, freshets
of African strings.

al-Andalus —
was it a dream,
a convivial dream, that tranquil
braid of Moors, Jews, and Gentiles?

al-Andalus —
the caliph's palaces conceived
as gardens,
the court poet's hope
an impregnable garden.

al-Andalus —
Saracen, pour the wine
from the colored ewer,
the moon-watched water
from the dipping cup.

al-Andalus —
Wake now with the white
cities of the Moors,
unassailable, alive within you,

the streets shimmering and absorbing —
the sultan's armies still bivouacked beneath
your now day-blessed brow.

Accept the sun's
regency and bribery,
Moorish gold.
Come to the window teeming
with ancient script, stone filigree,
for look, your room opens onto
a holy rampart.

As Iberian,
as Andalusian wine is sometimes
sweetened with southern fruit,
beyond the wolfish world,
let your impoverished eye —
Pauper,
where is your heaven? —
be freshened, ignited by the morning's
insouciant rose
and inescapable mimosa;
you live in a time
of kaleidoscopic fragrance:
let the lemons reach you, the little rain
on the baptizing lemons…

In the courtyard of the great mosque,
they are shaking fruit
from all the companionable trees,
and the Cordoban morning reveals:
Lieutenant, a column of do-or-die
trumpet lilies is your truce flag —

Take your freedom.
In the courtyard, breathe and become
the open-minded, washed-ashore pilgrim,
or the reveling, beguiled boy
who bolts from his father's arms
to conquer
a planet of fallen oranges.

Even the Lemons Know (Lessons)

In Seville, that grizzled week in spring,
I might have taken the hideaway sun
for a lover,
the rain was that insistent.

Then, dazzling, arrowy
as longed-for light,
you arrived to school me in
the helplessness which is love,
Jacinto —
ineluctable lesson —
the transparence —

Like a full wineskin,
or a cornucopia,
our deadsure coupling
is too potent,
too apparent to hide;
it's just as the incomparable
La Niña de los Peines sings:
Hasta los limones saben
que nos queremos los dos
("Even the lemons know
we're in love").

Remember, in Jerez de la Frontera,
Adán, the Argentine dancer, who grinned:
You must be lovers;
you have that glow.

He taught us the genesis of the tango,
that locked-in, libidinous dance —
how ebullient it felt
to learn the steps —
first executed by artful men
loitering in the raffish and sultry
brothels of Buenos Aires,
waiting their turn —
a dance that was flint-
hot, bracing as acrid wine, vicarious,
or not vicarious at all:
the agile, galvanized men
sometimes abandoning
the ruse of the woman
to be in the gallant
vise, the elegant
grip of another man...

The Soul in the Ruins of the Medina Azahara

And the green terraces checkered with ruins,
the inquisitive river whispers:
Carpenter, intoxicated dreamer,
what would you build for love?
Tell me, how would it counter
the wind's acumen,
the wind's artistry,
which is all honing, undoing?

Ten thousand laborers, a plethora
of never work-shy camels and mules,
twenty-five unstinting years to fashion
an unprecedented palace,
graced with the moniker
of the caliph's irreplaceable wife.
Erected in praise of her,
the barracks, the countless waterways,
the jammed markets
and redeeming mosques;
erected in praise,
the place of pure crystal
distilling rainbows,
the room with the colossal
bowl of mercury,
rocked by an odalisque,
hurling arrow-swift sunbeams to ensnare
the caliph's and his az-Zahar's laughter.

As love is frequently
ravaged or mislaid, recanted,
at its jubilee —
ornate, sumptuous, allied with desire —
the palace was wracked
by mercenaries.
And as you contemplate
the warriors' and the wind's pillage,
the ransacking years,
absorbing the myriad
nuances of the ruins,
answer the river,
the Guadalquivir:

What would you build for love,
carpenter, intoxicated singer?
What would you rather possess —
the ardor of the hard-dreaming caliph,
or the iridescent allure
of az-Zahar?
The wizardry of the glinting bowl of mercury,
or the sturdiness of the medina's
monumental gates?

Dove's Cry

There is a dove whose cry
is *not now, but simpler,*
and once we heard Juanillo
singing of that dove,
remember?
Teresita and Alícia had not yet been
lost in the crash.
It was the night of Iñaki's party.
In the pool, virile Esai and Tomás
held delicate Aicar on the surface —
the lithe tendrils of his floating hair
the color of bedstraw —
moving his limbs in unison,
so that his body seemed to open
like a remarkable starfish
or a winsome flower,
a very Hockney flower —

Like new bronze,
the partygoers, the sublime
women and men who seemed
the elating best of Andalusia,
each with their allotted
youth on earth,
their unrepeatable beauty —

that is meant, dear Lord, to be
weatherworn or broken? —

I woke in the hospital
with the lush, mitigating
memory of that night,
Juanillo's dove, the dream of fullness,

but this is the furious, impinging world:
the car swerves and rolls,
the life supports are relinquished —

There is a dove whose sorrow
is *God no, God no;*
there is a dove whose cry
is *not now, but simpler.*

The Flamenco Singer

He sings with the southernmost
heat of Cadiz,
listen,
in the ivy-quiet courtyard
under the Milky Way.

A thousand glittering blades
in his throat
mirror Sirius or Arcturus:
the distant, antediluvian fire
of the stars.

Now all the snowmen are melting
in Seville!

Black Sounds, Black Sounds (The Possessed)

Black sounds, black sounds —

And then the spirit of the deer
enters your audacious
flamenco, Jacinto,
your cells and sinews become
its luxury, its meadow —
its fleeting,
heaven-reaching horns
a candelabra —

so that if your heart were bared
it would be
the heart of a stag.

৵

The dark coins
of your nipples
in my mouth, the point-blank
fur of your chest, plush
as a meadow, restive,
the headlong, cogent hips, the brash
fire of our commingled breath
hushed for now:
voluminous hunger —
in the street of winds,
I devoured you
down to your beauty mark,

in the street of hurly-burly —
voluminous solace,
and at the core,
blameless delight,
all-out reverie — what I felt
as a sword-brandishing boy
captaining the commode,
as my fledgling brothers and I —
miniatures of the chivalrous
Three Musketeers —
aimed in unison —

                    Rapt
actors in a trance —
Jacinto, whatever possesses children?
Whatever possesses lovers?

Youth and animals
and black sounds...

Farruquito and La Niña

Here comes Farruquito
in his hydrant-colored shoes
and cummerbund,
bangs and hardy eyes of onyx —
mirroring your fleet gestures, Jacinto,
the mutiny your boots make
from the first to the arresting
seventh *olé;*

ecstatic, in deference, you doff
your dapper hat
to the excelling boy,
as he moves in a masterly
ribbon around you.

Flamenco on a flatbed truck,
candles ensconced
on a darkening hillside;
green strophes of cactus —
green, green as the frantic
leaves of heartbreak
the raw-spirited flamenco singer
rips and keeps re-ripping —

Now La Niña enters
the country of wounding guitars
and gypsy fillips,
with her never-torn, never-threadbare
white lace dress

and elfin gold hoops,
her lustrous braid,
her urchin-thin arm akimbo:

Isabel, in the Romany dusks,
in the dusks of castanets,
christened simply La Niña,
burnt umber girl
who is manna
to all who witness
her abracadabra poise:

little diligence,
little Doric of white fire...

The Way of Duende

Only mystery allows us to live,
only mystery.

LORCA

I. NIGHT MIND

The day mind gone, Lord,
and all the stringencies,
the day's bright yokes, the day's heavy
bridles of status:
flamenco as an impassioned
celebration of night,
of *duende*, of mystery's
warrens and arabesques —
Romans, Carthaginians, phantom
Moors wander through the redemptive,
incantatory dancing —
a séance enticing
the ghosts of many taciturn
olives, almonds, bulls
and sun-beaten hills,
an *adios* to the unjust heat,
when the lack-land, roistering gypsies seem
the green moon's and the falling star's
rightfully appointed heirs;
in zealous summer,
the most prosperous among us all.

II. NAKED

To see your back, gypsy,
your shaved torso,
naked in the zealous
summer heat,
your eyes a goading,
a dark and sober-sided blue I've found
only in Andalusia,
is to remember the rugged earth
swept clean of stallions,
reedless, futureless —
is to feel, Jacinto,
the tallow-pale quiet
of a runaway horse
at rest, the teeming,
swiftly marshalling silence
after the preening castanets —
taproot, crestfallen toad, hiding violet —
that same heart-lapping mystery,
that same stilling of the senses...

So Jacinto preens, cajoles, marshals
his expressive hips and boots
to sense *duende*
hidden in the darkest watermark,
the roguish wine stain
queering Juanillo's shirtfront —

What goblin wind, what glory
seizes him as he dances? —

Once, I swore, a piston-swift stag
had taken his place —

Tonight there is only the rakehell
laughter and torrential beauty,
the roar and daring
of unflappable *duende*
hard at work in the sudden
gusto of Jacinto,
as, in a flash,
Lorca's spirit is ensconced
at a corner table,
vibrant, vehement, applauding,
Lorca, the presiding god —

¿Donde está Jacinto?
Vanished, absconded,
his eagle-eaten heart
whisked over Andalusian meadows, estuaries —

Seville, stand on tiptoe,
or the river of his *duende*
will drown you —

67

Not drowning, not burial,
not avalanche, no:
duende caresses you
with what seem, at first,
mandarin-soft hands,
until they strike you:
Now I will make you, make you, make you
god-drunk, cliff-defying —

Suddenly the piquant, the enigmatic,
the sheerly authentic
suffuses the stage,
the authentic, death's consort:

Jacinto's dance steps, agile
then aggrieved, inconsolable —

What is it that makes us gasp?
What is it that makes us wait,
stock-still?

Flame coursing through us,
flame —

Dust devil, shadow king,
figure in a fever dream...

Galán de Noche

Our days in the grace of the Alhambra
are Moorish jasmine,
our nights sumptuous with nard
and the riveting flower dubbed
galán de noche.

Who is this star-governed "gallant"
whose outspokenness commands
our ennobling strolls in the story-rich
labyrinth of the Albaicín?

Gypsy, itinerant tailor,
make me a suit of its scent.

                ᘐ

In what garden,
by what equation,
is a virile man
a bloom?

If I asked Jacinto
I'm sure he'd proclaim,
Un hombre es canela y almizcle
("A man is cinnamon and musk"):
the tang of nutmeg,
not perfume —

But, so help me,
a man who sweetens the southern nights,
the four seasons,
with his strength and bonhomie,
his unfailing hope,
is a flower.

༄

Breath in the quietest
seedbeds of Granada,
breeze from the sierra,
tallying breeze,
don't let me forget:

a poet is a grieving lover, an elegist
for all he sees —

Brief emissary,
why make the leap,
when love's marauding power
means, in time:

Adiós, disheveled sheets,
bergamot and deep blue
shiver of morning glories;

adiós, galán de noche.

The Magician Lorca

So I took from you
a certain gypsy elixir,
so that I might likewise witness
a parliament of crickets,
swift angels of olive oil, the supreme
sun of a tuba,
unregenerate gypsy drums and numberless
crystal tambourines lacerating
the placid and dragonfly-delicate dawn —

With the wand of your words,
the mesmerizing wand,
I walked the unmonitored,
fairy tale groves
of poplars and holm oaks,
followed, heedful, spellbound, the fresh
garlands of rose and mulberry
that brighten the superannuated walls
of Granada;
felt the four points of the compass
flooding my unsnapped soul
all at once.

And the splendor of guardian sierras,
the jasmine of many courtyards
was given to me as a cake.

Taproot poet, in gratitude
for my partaking, for my being

the tagalong,
let me give you, in return,
white irises, broken nudes,
the still beguiling
bird mosaics of Italica,
a Sabbath of white horses
on Andalusian hills.

Keen magician, warlock of inmost
love and mystery,
let me give you back
the hoof-scarred plain's glory,
the indefatigable bullfighter's brio,
the unabraded fire in my hands.

Little Ballad of the Moorish White Town

for Lorca

On the winding way to the far-lying white town,
rider,
the upraised, the ferrymen cactuses
are green hands:
the day is an exodus
through green hands —

First, the wind-swayed fields
in mist,
then the summit,
like an owl-white ship:

Arcos de la Frontera,

a tranquil place, poised
on a gargantuan limestone
promontory — all of it
agreeably white,
save the window grills,
the prodigal black of your boots,
save the brisk red
of rugged pomegranates
a stringer of vying boys steal
for soccer balls,
the red of a single
geranium on a sill.

꒜

Don't go to Arcos
in the heat of summer, I said.
Don't try to settle the score,
Caco.
I know he's your brother,
but don't go,

꒜

for death is the black, tethered ram
that waits;

death is the old women of Arcos,
night-shawled, implacable, singing
I'm jealous of the river
that reflects your face,
as they beat the ready olives
from the branches
with insistent canes.

꒜

At sundown, at soccer's end,
an uproarious
salvo of ruby seeds.

Then, above the Moorish promontory,
the lime-washed streets,
pale as the priest's cheese,
the moon's lashless eye —

In the windstruck field, suddenly,
your headfirst silence —

Your brother Joaquin washes
his crimson chest,
his quitclaim stiletto,
and the startled river,
the Guadalete,
has no breastplate against
this swift decree of red.

꒰

On the winding way to the remote
white town,
the night is an exodus
through green hands:

in the moon-sweep,
the saddle is cool
as the reddened river,
and the pliant bay meant
to carry you back,
riderless, riderless…

Catechism in the Garden of Five Pines

for Lorca

Sh! The old women from Villalba del Alcor
are talking.
When brusque soldiers came,
tiny sisters, they hid
behind a stand of bearded irises
like chivalrous *señors*.

What is time to the women,
what is memory?

In their garden of five pines,
the years pass,
further and further away
from Franco.
The sibilant fountain,
the unremitting spring, has no sense
of civil war;
the cradling earth, the clear water
are no longer colored by chaos,
the crimson of many Cains and Abels.

And where has the blood gone?
Is the blood ever stanched?
Not the blood
but the spirit of the blood
teems, still percolates
beneath Iberian ground,
still troubles the indomitable sisters,
the eyewitness galaxies of olives.

Why weren't the olives
a shield,
silver-green, or a gauntlet,
when stealthy fascists intrigued
to murder the poet?

Mute to the human,
the trees had no sway,
no dominion over
the undeterred pistols,
they could only lament to the persistent
altar candle of the summer moon:
Hands and arms for what?

Lord, Lord, my unflagging
blacksmith and maker,
for what unrivaled aim,
for what annealing reason
was I forged?

You have hands to minister
and receive manna;
you have arms to clasp
the larkish solace of children,
ears to absorb
the world's rumors,
to incorporate
the telltale, the human.

And if the news of the human brings me
only terror,
if the news of the human
is only havoc?
In the garden of five pines,

the years pass
but not the rumors, the harrowing
reports of the poet's end:
in a *barranco*, a bleak gully,
at the last,
a bullet in his backside
for loving men —
Is the world that broken-toothed,
that brutal?

The world is justice-starved, vast,
its kings incorrigible,
and fear is the aphrodisiac:
Beware! Beware! the poet cried.
This life is not a dream!

Poet, lodestar,
lover of men —
I am love! I am nature! —
wounded seer,
is it only in genial dreams
that freedom lives?
Is it real
the road to paradise?

Like Isis in Andalusia,
resolute, you'll follow the roads
I revered
through the raven-dark field
where the moon roams,
unpersecuted, seeking
the little paradise of the Tamarit,
treasurable orchard

where I dreamed without end —
unerring, you'll embrace
the fecund plain
where I veered, blindfolded
but never effaced.

In the knockabout, warring world,
what will I face?
A gag or a blindfold?
Will my freedom
be stripped from me?
In the garden of five pines now,
tell me,
what is the worst?
What is the worst
that can happen?

More terrible than the heart's carnage,
to walk the road to paradise
as if the road were leprous,
to journey, immutable,
a flat-worlder, a trudging sleepwalker
in realms of jasmine,
precincts of showy verbena,
wandering scornfully amid
pealing bells, ringing anvils,
voluptuous pageantry,
forever reticent or stony, forever
gutted or stuffed with straw:
at each anniversary,
in every season, an impassive
stranger on this earth.

Gypsy Wedding

In the grave-eyed time after
my father's cancer,
to help me to live
("*ayudarte a vivir*"), Jacinto took me
to a gypsy wedding.

First, a headlong accordion,
a breakneck clarinet
enraptured us.

There were fresh-cut sunflowers,
trumpet lilies,
coursing then vanishing wine,
sweet mayhem as a coaxable ram
climbed a gaily painted ladder
to untrammeled applause,
night-singing crickets at the moon's zenith —

But what I prized most,
beyond the bride
in dogwood white,
was how the father of the bow-tied,
extravagantly bare-chested groom
smoothed his firstborn's
sweat-soaked hair
with a marvelous, sun-roughened hand:
Ah, fatherhood —

Gypsies, fathers, rams,
help me to live.

PART III

～

More Than Peace and Cypresses

Sons and Violets

I. THE TREEHOUSE

A cancer-wracked dreamer's gambit,
an old man's folly,
this eleventh-hour carpentry:
here are the vivacious branches,
the buoyant dream;
here is the not-defeated child's applause —

I know the version that fueled
and failed me:
my life was ruined
by a pirate-priest, a cyclops,
and I roamed the world,
heart-gutted, demolishing,
secretly demolished,
his cat's-paw,
his crippled ward.

In heaven's name, if I am dying,
surely I can choose
another version:
the power of alchemy
or deft scissors —
isn't that the splendid chess, the secret
freedom of the dead?

And what about forgiveness?
As my sons have forgiven me
my unremitting anger,

at the end of life,
the soul's bow and exit,
isn't it the truest solace
to be able to say,
like a sated actor, even
to your nemesis,
your worst bane:
It was so beautiful to live
when you lived.

I guide my studious eldest son
up the laddered oak,
and acquaint him with delight,
all systems *go* —
in the treetop sometimes whistling
a bit of Fats Domino,
a bit of "Blue Rondo à la Turk,"
as a heart's cartwheel, a little broom-
sweep in a hard luck time.

The leaves part,
a green homecoming,
and a dead priest's hushing hand
is all the comfort in the world,
and the unbetraying gems of his eyes mean
only laughter, laughter.

II. WHAT DOES FAMILY MEAN?

Over the moat of the unspeakable, the unspoken,
we've eased down the drawbridge,
my cancer-caught father and I,
for I have been a cupped palm, a calyx
for his cauterizing tears,
his long-in-blooming
lotus of apology.
And I know if I reached
boldly into his burly chest,
like an avid and undaunted bell ringer,
I'd find, not a hangman's knot,
but the *is, is, is*
of an at-the-ready heart...

Where once an iron sadness prevailed,
now courage is a tenant
in my father's shipshape house,
and an unaccustomed peace.
Dismay, like the cobwebbed husk
of a crusading knight,
is consigned
to the jammed and cavernous garage,
and for both of us, it seems,
love's Quixote's quest
is for thrilling speech.

In the quickening, urgent days
of my father's time-at-hand,
my mother is a touchstone, a holiday,
and a restoring stranger

all at once.
And when I listen ardently, intently,
as my mother speaks,
the allaying pressure of my hand
an *aide-mémoire*, I know
my passion and purpose on earth,
how, by and by, the riveting tale becomes
the never-jaded listener's
glorious onus.

In the wind of the century's end,
what does family mean —
beyond storehoused wisdom and bridgeable pain,
beyond adjacent dreams, consequences?

Part of what I know is:
at first gaze, my mother's hazel eyes
and bloodwarm breasts
were a berceuse,
my father's steadying hand
the beginning of reverence,
and like a magus,
unimpeded, I would lift
the cancer from his lungs,
if I had the power.

All day fighting to dispel the indelible
dream of my father's death —
a dream of doleful nurses, doctors
surrounding me,
beginning to sing,
a downcast circle —
so nothing readied me
for the deer's breakneck leap
across the beltway.
Before I could protest,
the car crumpled — the wild
web of the air bag gripping me:
the white curtain I'd feared
since childhood:
an avalanche,
an atomic flash —
arrow-sure,
it finds you, it finds you,
the taut, unsayable
end you fear.

No, nothing readied me
to be counted, marked
as one of the mortal ones —
the ill-wind wreath of the antlers,
the ensuing scar, an elfin
river on my ring finger —
one of the quick, imperiled animals.

In short time,
his real death came:
the flurry of paramedics,
and my unstinting brother
righting my father's body,
at cancer's end, jewel-still,
and the riveting flatline:
sign of the self
once more maverick, unravaged;
my father calling, in a waking dream,
as if through riffling wind:

Did you forget?
This flesh is changeable
as air, as fire;
this flesh is swift and fleeting
and flyapart...

IV. OH

My father didn't want a funeral,
a garish coffin or a grave;
I was relieved,
but that still meant the task
of being the able emcee
at his memorial.

At the cat-quiet end
of the formal program —
Fatherless, I thought.
What will it mean? —
I summoned my father's friends —
pilots, airmen —
to the podium, discovering
that in the stringent fifties
my father helped desegregate
student quarters at West Point
by dauntlessly insisting
on rooming with a white cadet.

And for more than an hour
the eloquent airmen came,
munificent quilters with transfixing
swatches of my father's life.

You see, a son grows
in the weather of his father's
wounds and triumphs,
without maps or discernible keys,
without signposts or even
the simplest facts:

a father, to the end,
an inspiriting mystery —
Son, freestanding son,
someday the hidden
carnage in your father's heart
will be brought to anointing light,
someday, someday, inheritor —
an undoubtable jigsaw
to be pieced,
the Gethsemanes and glories,
the clues and colors scattered:

oh and *oh* and *oh* ...

V. THE APPOINTMENT

No earth can contain
my feeling for you, Father,
no earth, no chalice,
no finite form.

Let me ponder
in matchless tranquility,
uninterruptible peace,
the maze of bigotry,
of shame and dismaying silence,
the waylaying maze
that keeps us blunderers bereft
of the fabled tree of knowledge,
its pendant, invigorating fruit,
sunlit and moonlit,
full of God's elegance.

Like the Nazarene
or a nimble adept,
now envision a dulcet,
a jubilant appointment
in a garden place
unbossed by the illusion,
the mirage of time:

I promise I will meet you there
in that neverending present.

VI. TO WIN THE YOUNG GOD BACK AGAIN

In the farseeing, revising dream the diminishing
cancer was gone;
he was restored to me
at last, galvanizing, vibrant,
a cloud-wrapped ace,
for in the afterlife
my pilot father appeared
to be maybe thirty.
I blessed my good fortune:
How did I win
the young god back again?
I basked in his memorable
bronze and black gaze,
his high-flying verve,
though in time he waved me away
with a delicate
Noli me tangere,
and I understood
he was schoolbound:
he was studying to be,
in the next life,
a Nobel-winning mathematician:
not one to do anything by halves,
my father!

Long ago I stopped asking
what happens after death;
all the ordinary losses
marred the question,
as if with blackout paper
or barbed wire.

Today I woke suffused
with calm, strangely certain
of the self's survival,
strangely certain,
as a friend proposed,
everyone survives everything.

Go on studying, Father.
If I could I would smooth
your newfound uniform of numbers...

VII. SONS AND VIOLETS

for Sean,
after Attilio Bertolucci

In the hush-a-bye woods, in a time
that will never be over,
your father caught you,
dozing hobo-light in a truant
bed of violets,
and fashioned a thin
belittling switch
to whip you for the womanish
place you'd hidden.

Now grown men, what we want is
a leave-the-boy-be love: violets
gathered with the patience
that suddenly grips a boy's core
when the time comes
for the task —
patience as inchoate,
as secret as the violet
as it waits beneath
a showy carpet of topaz
and carnelian leaves —

Grown at last, what we want is
violets in profusion
to fashion memorial bouquets;
the only flower
the close-to-mendicant woods

have to offer this rapacious season
to win the young gods
back again, to venerate
our virile and exacting fathers
who died too young,
too careworn —
who are eagerly reborn in us now,
as we bend,
intent on beauty,
recalling a boy's unbridled pleasure
in a live-a-little bed of color:

supplicants,
sons and archers, with the first-prize
arrows of our concentration.

More Than Peace and Cypresses

More than peace and cypresses, emboldened
hares at the field's edge,

Father, I love
gallantry, tenacity, the sanguine

heart before the ledge:
the artist questing and failing —

the feet of bested Icarus
plunging into the sea's crest —

the artist triumphing: a page of fire
from the book of heroes.

More than light-hooved gazelles, views
from the mizzenmast,

enlivening shores,
more than soldier-still lilies, I love

the torchlike men who've taught me —
past the rueful

glitter of lucre and guns,
past the starkness of the lynching tree —

the truth-or-bust beauty
of passion transformed

into sheer compassion,
true shouldering,

and common as breath, common as breath,
the extravagant wheel of birth and death.

About the Author

Cyrus Cassells is the author of three previous books, *The Mud Actor*, *Soul Make a Path Through Shouting*, and *Beautiful Signor*. Among his honors are a Lannan Literary Award, a Lambda Literary Award, and the William Carlos Williams Award. An Associate Professor of English at Texas State University–San Marcos, he has served on the Board of Directors of the Austin Circle of Theaters and garnered a 2003 B. Iden Payne Award nomination for Outstanding Featured Actor in a Drama for his role as Fielding in August Wilson's *Jitney*. In his devotion to the work of Lorca, he was a dramaturg for a production of *Blood Wedding*. From 1991 to 1997 he lived primarily in Florence and Rome. Since 1999 he has spent a part of each year in Paris.

*Copper Canyon Press wishes to acknowledge the support of
Lannan Foundation in funding the publication and distribution
of exceptional literary works.*

LANNAN LITERARY SELECTIONS 2004

Marvin Bell, *Rampant*

Cyrus Cassells, *More Than Peace and Cypresses*

Ben Lerner, *The Lichtenberg Figures*

Joseph Stroud, *Country of Light*

Eleanor Rand Wilner, *The Girl with Bees in Her Hair*

LANNAN LITERARY SELECTIONS 2000–2003

John Balaban, *Spring Essence:
The Poetry of Hồ Xuân Hương*

Hayden Carruth, *Doctor Jazz*

Norman Dubie, *The Mercy Seat:
Collected & New Poems,
1967–2001*

Sascha Feinstein, *Misterioso*

James Galvin, *X: Poems*

Jim Harrison, *The Shape of the
Journey: New and Collected Poems*

Maxine Kumin, *Always Beginning:
Essays on a Life in Poetry*

Antonio Machado, *Border of a
Dream: Selected Poems*, trans-
lated by Willis Barnstone

W.S. Merwin, *The First Four Books
of Poems*

Cesare Pavese, *Disaffections:
Complete Poems 1930–1950*,
translated by Geoffrey Brock

Antonio Porchia, *Voices*,
translated by W.S. Merwin

Kenneth Rexroth, *The Complete
Poems of Kenneth Rexroth*,
edited by Sam Hamill and
Bradford Morrow

Alberto Ríos, *The Smallest Muscle
in the Human Body*

Theodore Roethke, *On Poetry
& Craft*

Ann Stanford, *Holding Our Own:
The Selected Poems of Ann
Stanford*, edited by Maxine
Scates and David Trinidad

Ruth Stone, *In the Next Galaxy*

Rabindranath Tagore, *The Lover
of God*, translated by Tony K.
Stewart and Chase Twichell

*Reversible Monuments: Contemporary
Mexican Poetry*, edited by
Mónica de la Torre and
Michael Wiegers

César Vallejo, *The Black Heralds*,
translated by Rebecca
Seiferle

C.D. Wright, *Steal Away: Selected
and New Poems*

For more on the Lannan Literary Selections, visit:
www.coppercanyonpress.org

The Chinese character for poetry is made up of two parts: "word" and "temple." It also serves as pressmark for Copper Canyon Press.

Founded in 1972, Copper Canyon Press remains dedicated to publishing poetry exclusively, from Nobel laureates to new and emerging authors. The Press thrives with the generous patronage of readers, writers, booksellers, librarians, teachers, students, and funders — everyone who shares the conviction that poetry invigorates the language and sharpens our appreciation of the world.

THE ALLEN FOUNDATION *for* THE ARTS

NATIONAL
ENDOWMENT
FOR THE ARTS

THE
STARBUCKS
FOUNDATION

WASHINGTON
STATE ARTS
COMMISSION

Major funding has been provided by:

The Allen Foundation for The Arts

Lannan Foundation

National Endowment for the Arts

The Starbucks Foundation

Washington State Arts Commission

For information and catalogs:
COPPER CANYON PRESS
Post Office Box 271
Port Townsend,
Washington 98368
360/385-4925
www.coppercanyonpress.org

The text is set in Californian with titles set in Goudy Village. Both fonts are based on typefaces designed by Frederic Goudy in the 1930s. Book design and composition by Valerie Brewster, Scribe Typography. Printed on archival-quality Glatfelter Author's Text at McNaughton & Gunn, Inc.